MACHINE LEARNING

An In-Depth Beginners Guide into the Essentials of
Machine Learning Algorithms

PETER van DIJCK

Copyright Notice.

Table of Contents

CHAPTER 1: INTRODUCTION TO MACHINE LEARNING

Machine learning is a method of data analysis that automates analytical model building. Using algorithms that iteratively learn from data, machine learning allows computers to find hidden insights without being explicitly programmed where to look.

Algorithm - it is no longer an unknown term for many of us, and today, algorithms exist in every aspect of computer science. Algorithms are widely used in different outperforming fields such as social media, e-commerce, transportation, healthcare, education, etc. With the growing technology trends, algorithms these days are considered as the key building blocks for Machine Learning (ML) and Artificial Intelligence (AI).

An algorithm is a sequence of instructions, which eventually confirms the successful completion of a particular task. Being humans, we apply algorithms to perform some actions in every aspect of our daily lives.

The algorithm makes us break anything into small steps, for an easy and effective understanding of the complex things. For example, on a fine morning when you are ready to leave the office, and you can't recollect where the car keys are. How would you find them? One smart approach might be the application of an algorithm, which is a sequential procedure to locate the answer (keys) quickly.

At first, you will look at the places where you usually drop the keys. Next, you will recollect the last occasion when you have used them. Later, you will check the first room where you went, when you have entered the home. Eventually, by the flow of steps, you will find the car keys. Thus, the knowledge of algorithm stands to be a valued asset for enlightening our daily lives or even the lives of others. With algorithms, there is no limit for us to imagine, and making them real.

Benefits of using Algorithms.

There are numerous benefits of using algorithms in both our personal and professional lives, which becomes impractical to explain all of them in a single article. However, some of them are explained below.

You can transform any complicated thing into an algorithm, which will help you in the decision-making process.

Instead of creating a to-do list, you can write an algorithm to prioritize your daily tasks.

Based on your preferences and historical data, you can write an algorithm to get recommendations on what genre films to watch.

You can write an algorithm to foresee the best available time for you to go on a vacation.

Nowadays, machine learning is a popular word, generally about artificial intelligence and big data. But have any idea what precisely it is? It is artificial intelligence's sub-set where computer algorithms are utilized for learning data and information autonomously. Machine learning computers have the ability to change and enhance their algorithms all by themselves.

It's completely about listing computers in the job of sorting via huge amount of data which modern technology has enabled us to produce (also known as Big Data). Its prime focus is on the growth of computer programs which can teach themselves for emerging and changing when unveiled to new data.

Essentiality of Machine Learning:

Presently, computers are enabled by machine learning algorithms to interact with humans, find terrorist suspects, write and publish sport match reports and drive cars autonomously. This will influence many industries and the jobs within them, and for this purpose, every manager must have some grasp at least of what machine learning is and how it is developing.

Currently, it is possible for automatically and quickly creating models which can analyze more complex and bigger data and supply more relevant and faster results in fact on a larger scale. And by producing exact models, a company has a better opportunity to identify profitable chances or ignoring strange risks.

How IoT can advantage from Machine Learning.

IoT machines are producing a massive amount of data and machine learning is completely being employed for analyzing and reading that data to help enhance client service and efficiency, and lessen energy consumption and costs. For producing a good learning system, you require:

Ensemble modeling

Scalability

Iterative and automation process

Basic and advanced algorithms

Data preparation capabilities

Air quality and energy with Machine Learning:

Air quality and several types of energy consumption implement artificial intelligence, cloud computing and big data for mapping nonlinear and complex air pollution trends effectively and relevantly. The technique employs deep machine learning and provides intelligent tips to managers and users on saving energy and getting better air quality. Now the solutions can be suggested automatically, thanks to this technology. In fact, the equipment can be identified from a single metering point.

For getting the most value from machine learning, you should know about pairing the best algorithms with the correct processes and tools. Albeit this is one of the largest trends to detect everything and anything nowadays, more research needs to be done for testing the algorithms.

In today's competitive world, every organization tries to outsmart its competitors to gain market share and improve the bottom line. They are constantly looking for new strategies and techniques to achieve this objective. Machine learning is the new buzz word that has caught the attention of the organizations. Machine learning is a type of artificial intelligence that is related to the patterns and study of certain systems that use huge input of data for its working. Here are the four things about this naive technique.

Complex pattern recognition - It has one of the most important features that it can be used to study and understand complex patterns in the data. It helps to give meaning to the data by providing a relationship and quantifying the same. This feature eliminates irrelevant data from the huge chunk of data and you are left with pure relevant data that can be used to dig out various useful insights. It also helps the user to understand primary and secondary variables for a set of information. This helps in the pre-processing technique and acceleration process.

Ability to take intelligent decisions - The process can take decisions with or without the guidance of a user. It is a type of artificial intelligence which makes decisions based on the input and the desired output. It selects the best optimum choice from a given set of options which will benefit the user as compared to the other neglected choices.

Self-Improving and Modifying: Suppose you teach in a Math class, who will you prefer as a student; a kid who makes the same mistake again and again or a kid who corrects his last mistake and improves next time? Your answer will more likely be the later one as it reduces your efforts by a great deal. Same is the case here. It has the characteristic of improving the standards of its decision-making ability and modifies itself for better; enhanced outputs benefit the user to a greater extent. It refines itself with multiple iterations on a particular problem and provides the user with an optimum solution.

Adds power to your analytics: Machine learning enhances the power of analytics. Consumer behavior is dynamic and changes constantly. It is important to tap and respond to these changes. It optimizes complex goals and improves lifetime value of the customers. It helps in building new predictive models to nullify the change. Another important characteristic is that it helps to track the process of a particular campaign right from the start of the campaign and not wait till the campaign ends.

Machine learning algorithms are often categorized as being supervised or unsupervised. Supervised algorithms require humans to provide both input and desired output, in addition to furnishing feedback about the accuracy of predictions during training. Once training is complete, the algorithm will apply what was learned to new data. Unsupervised algorithms do not need to be trained with desired outcome data. Instead, they use an iterative approach called deep learning to review data and arrive at conclusions. Unsupervised learning algorithms are used for more complex processing tasks than supervised learning systems.

The processes involved in machine learning are similar to that of data mining and predictive modeling. Both require searching through data to look for patterns and adjusting program actions accordingly. Many people are familiar with machine learning from shopping on the internet and being served ads related to their purchase. This happens because recommendation engines use machine learning to personalize online ad delivery in almost real time. Beyond personalized marketing, other common machine learning use cases include fraud detection, spam filtering, network security threat detection, predictive maintenance and building news feeds.

Facebook's News Feed, for example, uses machine learning to personalize each member's feed. If a member frequently stops scrolling to read or "like" a particular friend's posts, the News Feed will start to show more of that friend's activity earlier in the feed. Behind the scenes, the software is simply using statistical analysis and predictive analytics to identify patterns in the user's data and use those patterns to populate the News Feed. Should the member no longer stop to read, like or comment on the friend's posts, that new data will be included in the data set and the News Feed will adjust accordingly?

Sources

It has become possible for you to get machine learning when you search online. It can be known as an intelligent stage where devices are doing all individual steps. Well, there are considerations that you need to do to be able to buy it. It is your important analysis that you need to make if you wish to get the best service provider. If you can take excellent steps in the best way, then it would prove to be the best one that would add a big smile of satisfaction to your face. So, it is important for you to make sure that right efforts are taken to get some of your time so that it would prove to be very important to you. Once you take all important steps, it would not lead to any worry.

* Look for their services: You have to make sure that right efforts are made to get the best source that would prove to be the best one for you. It is important to make sure that it also provides the best remedy for you that would prove to be the right one for you. You have to ensure that that you try to get in getting in touch with that would help you to feel great for your choice. If you can get the best one that would be useful, then you should try to make a good appointment.

* Check their technology: It is also important to make sure that right efforts are made to look at their technological innovation that would help you get the best idea whether it would be able to anticipate the best one for you. It should be able to provide you with the best one that would not lead to any worry at all. This

would help you to feel the best for your ultimate choice that has been taken by you.

* Get the best services: You need to make sure that you get the right services with the help of digital reasoning for you. With the help of the best source, you would be able to find that right steps are taken in a good way. Thus it is your own choice that would prove to be the best one making it possible to get the right one.

Machine Learning, Edge Computing, and Serverless are the three key technologies that will redefine the Cloud Computing platforms.

Machine Learning (ML) is becoming an integral part of modern applications. From the web to mobile to IoT, ML is powering the new breed of applications through natural user experiences and inbuilt intelligence.

After virtualization and containerization, Serverless is emerging as the next wave of computing services. Serverless or Functions as a Service (FaaS) attempts to simplify the developer experience by minimizing the operational overhead in deploying and managing code. Contemporary applications designed as micro services are built on top of Faas platforms like AWS Lambda, Azure Functions, Google Cloud Functions, and Open Whisk.

Edge Computing takes computer closer to the applications. Each edge location mimics the public cloud by exposing a compatible set of services and endpoints that the applications can consume. It is all set to redefine enterprise infrastructure.

These three emerging technologies - Serverless, Edge Computing and Machine Learning - will be the key technology drivers for the next generation of infrastructure. The objective of this article is to explain how developers will benefit from the combination of these technologies.

The availability of data, ample storage capacity, and sufficient computing power are essential for implementing Machine Learning. Cloud becomes the natural fit for dealing with Machine Learning. Data Scientists are relying on the cloud for ingesting and storing massive data sets. They are also using pay-as-you-go infrastructure for processing and analyzing the data. With cheaper storage and advanced computing platforms powered by GPUs and FPGAs, the cloud is fast becoming the destination for building complex ML models.

At a high level, there are three steps involved in building ML-based applications. The first phase is training an algorithm with existing data. The second phase is validating the outcome for accuracy with test data. These two steps are repeated till the expected accuracy is achieved by the algorithm. With each iteration, the algorithm learns more about the data and finds new patterns, which will increase the efficiency. What comes out of these two steps is referred to a Machine Learning model, which is carefully tuned to work with new data points. The third and final step is invoking the model with production data to achieve the expected outcome, which may be based on prediction, classification, or grouping of new data.

The first two phases involving ML require heavy lifting, which is tackled by the cloud. The training and test data is stored in cloud storage while the special class of virtual machines is utilized for tuning the algorithm. The interesting fact is that the final, evolved model of ML doesn't need many resources. It is a piece of code that contains the parameters obtained from the previous two phases based on rigorous training and validation. For many scenarios, this model can be embedded within an application as a standalone entity. Based on the predefined parameters, it will analyze new data points as they get generated. When the production dataset submitted to the model becomes significantly different from what is expected, the need for retraining the algorithm arises. At this point, a new model is evolved after repeating the testing and training phases. The updated model is then redeployed to the applications to handle the production datasets.

From an operations standpoint, generating ML models requires provisioning and configuring a variety of storage and compute resources. DevOps teams are involved in managing the infrastructure necessary for this task. The Ops team will have to ensure that the evolved model is delivered to the applications. Each model may be tracked and maintained through a versioning mechanism. Finally, the model should be made available to developers consuming it in their applications. This is where Serverless platforms play a vital role in simplifying the DevOps cycle.

Even though a Machine Learning model is generated in the cloud, it may not be invoked in the cloud. For most scenarios, the model should be kept close to applications. For example, a predictive maintenance model generated to detect malfunctioning of a connected car needs to be closer to the automobile than running in the cloud. These models are typically pushed to the edge of the Cloud Computing layer. Similar to a Content Delivery Network (CDN) that caches static content and video streams across multiple points of presence, the ML model needs to be hosted across multiple locations within an edge network. Applications will invoke the ML model that's closest to their location. This reduces the latency by avoiding the round trip to the cloud. Since the DevOps teams are responsible for pushing the latest ML model across multiple edge locations, they can automate the process of upgrading the model.

At each edge location, the ML model is deployed as a Serverless function, which is invoked by applications. Since the unit of deployment in FaaS is a function, it is far more efficient than pushing a heavy virtual machine or a container. Each time a new ML model is evolved, a new version is assigned to it and pushed across all the locations. This makes the process less error prone and efficient.

Unconventional knowledge about Machine Learning

Concentrate on feature engineering!

Imagine a given data set from which you have to create an algorithm to create certain outputs by which certain decisions will be made. For example, imagine a data set containing the specific times when each employee enters the office, leaves for lunch, comes back and leaves for home. By these, we have to find out the employee who spends the most time in office and award him/her the best employee award.

But, the specific times or a pair of specific times or so will not be able to provide enough data to create an algorithm for this. Now, if you can create a new data set which contains the summation of time duration which the employee spends in office between coming and going for lunch and then coming back from lunch and going to the office, we can easily create an algorithm to test the said condition.

This is known as feature engineering and the maximum time is to be spent on this to create better algorithms which are flexible and require lesser bug fixing.

More data and a simpler algorithm is better than a complicated, clever algorithm

It is a proven fact that once the input fields are defined, there is only a limited amount of analytic variations that you can perform with the algorithm. Having a simpler algorithm with a better flexibility for addition and variation along with a large data set is always beneficial to create incredibly powerful classifiers with increasing data load.

Learn variations in models

Learn multiple classifiers with random data subsets to create more powerful models of machine learning. There is a possibility that there is a little loss in interpretability due to the varying sequence in models for the final prediction, but making the application performance sensitive will increase your power to compensate for the loss of interpretability.

Do not be oversimplified at the cost of accuracy

To quote Occam's razor, "plurality is not to be posited without necessity." In simpler terms, if a particular problem has two solutions, the simpler one is more effective. In machine learning, however, this hypothesis should not be used extensively. At many places in machine learning, algorithms with additional complexity can benefit with more performance. In short, prefer simple models for their ease and quickness of fitting along with better interpretability but never be blind enough to be sure that they will lead to better performance.

Correlation does not necessarily mean causation

When modeling observable data the correlation between two variables can come out to be definite, but this will not necessarily tell us 'why?' And until you know the 'why' you cannot conclude a causative relation. Just because it is visualized that the presence of one thing is also in the presence of another thing, it does not mean the presence of the thing is because of the other thing. Machine learning will go a long way in changing the technological world in ways we cannot imagine right now. Organizations are now considering machine learning as their core research areas and the next 'internet' of the future. Getting trained in machine learning through books or Machine Learning courses will go a long way in skyrocketing individual's careers.

CHAPTER 2: MACHINE LEARNING APPLICATION

Most industries working with large amounts of data have recognized the value of machine learning technology. By gleaning insights from this data – often in real time – organizations can work more efficiently or gain an advantage over competitors.

Financial services

Banks and other businesses in the financial industry use machine learning technology for two key purposes: to identify important insights in data, and prevent fraud. The insights can identify investment opportunities, or help investors know when to trade. Data mining can also identify clients with high-risk profiles, or use cyber surveillance to pinpoint warning signs of fraud.

Government

Government agencies such as public safety and utilities have a particular need for machine learning since they have multiple sources of data that can be mined for insights. Analyzing sensor data, for example, identifies ways to increase efficiency and save money. Machine learning can also help detect fraud and minimize identity theft

Healthcare.

Machine learning is a fast-growing trend in the health care industry, thanks to the advent of wearable devices and sensors that can use data to assess a patient's health in real time. The technology can also help medical experts analyze data to identify trends or red flags that may lead to improved diagnoses and treatment.

Marketing and sales

Websites recommending items you might like based on previous purchases are using machine learning to analyze your buying history – and promote other items you'd be interested in. This ability to capture data, analyze it and use it to personalize a shopping experience (or implement a marketing campaign) is the future of retail.

Oil and gas

Finding new energy sources. Analyzing minerals in the ground, Predicting refinery sensor failure, Streamlining oil distribution to make it more efficient and cost-effective. The number of machine learning use cases for this industry is vast – and still expanding.

Transportation

Analyzing data to identify patterns and trends is key to the transportation industry, which relies on making routes more efficient and predicting potential problems to increase profitability. The data analysis and modeling aspects of machine learning are important tools to delivery companies, public transportation, and other transportation organizations.

Automated Forex Trading systems do have advantages over manual human trading. The automated trading system can monitor the Forex markets 24 hours a day; automated systems are completely disciplined to the set of system rules and never stray; automated trading systems are immune to greed and fear and emotion never influences their trading decisions; automated Forex systems always follow the money management rules defined by the user. However, it is apparently very ironic that these basic principles that define the strengths of a system are also many times its downfall. Forex robots cannot 'analyze' the market price action like a human being. Therefore, Forex Robots Enter Every Trade that meets a defined set of conditions. Human Traders Most Often Do Not!

Prevailing sentiment contends that, out of all Forex traders, only a small percentage are successful long term. The referenced figures vary depending on the source cited, but the percentages consistently average in the 5% to 8% range. In alignment with this figure, very few Forex robots survive the tests of live account Forex trading, with a mere 1% to 2% surviving more than a few months before their rule-sets becoming obsolete, and the losses begin piling up. The ideal solution is obvious. Combine the discipline and tireless availability of an automated Forex robot with the savvy and experience of a successful human trader.

It is in this vein that much of the groundbreaking research on algorithmic Forex trading lies. By utilizing machine learning to 'teach' an algorithm certain prevailing 'human' decisions that affect trade entry, existing systems for trading Forex automatically can be converted. Some research shows that training entry tactics with machine learning strategies (Genetic Programming and Neural Networks to name a few) do significantly improve the performance of systems on out-of-sample data. These conclusions lend some early credibility to the notion of Forex trading using machine learning.

The concept that we discuss here departs from this strategy in that we use the learning technologies to train sets of 'humanized' data as opposed to raw data before a condition. By utilizing these datasets, the learning becomes 'why did the human enter this trade?' vs. 'do the raw data support entering a trade right now?' When the learning begins to focus on more abstract data, the resulting systems tend to become more robust or tend to work better in varying market conditions than those that simply attempt to identify winning Forex trades from raw indicator data. The concept is that basic indicator conditions trigger a trade Set-Up, for instance, a fast moving average crosses a slower moving average. The learning algorithm then works to filter these set-ups using the training it acquired from human training datasets. The automated trading system says, "Based on what I've learned from my expert human teacher, does this set-up look like a good deal?" Instead of, "The computational result using all of the empirical data is greater than the defined variable, get in or out?"

A machine learning business could very well be your best opportunity as an IT professional. That's because this unique area of the computer world is one that requires a great deal of specialized skill to navigate while at the same time being an essential part of much consumer computer activity. In other words, it's necessary, but there are only so many people who can do it.

Not surprisingly, you can see how being able to bridge the gap and allowing companies to make use of machine learning to drive their business would make your services extremely valuable. That's why, if you're looking to start an online internet business and you have the necessary knowledge, then machine learning could be the perfect field for you.

So what exactly is machine learning and why is it so valuable in the online business world? Simply put, it is a method of data analysis that uses algorithms that learn from data and produce specific results without being specifically programmed to do so. These algorithms can analyze data, calculate how frequently certain parts of it are used and generate responses based on these calculations to interact with users automatically.

In fact, machine learning is used in some capacities in today's world, from generating those "other items you may be interested in" responses at sites like Amazon, to providing fraud detection, to generating web search results and filtering spam in e-mail servers. These are just a few of the common applications of this process, all of which can be extremely important to companies for driving business.

By using machine learning, companies can personalize their customer's experience, make sure that the right products are being put in front of them at the right time and ensure that their company is coming up in web searches to reach the largest possible audience of potential customers. With your own machine learning business, you can step in and help them to achieve these ends.

The one common factor in all of the applications of machine learning is that while the connection from point A to point B may seem obvious, actually getting there can be like reading ancient Greek. If you don't know what you're looking at, you won't be able to get very far. So companies will be all too eager to employ someone who can find their way through this thorny path and get the results they want.

By playing up how you can use machine learning to help their company and positioning yourself as the best possible option for handling this end of business technology, you'll be creating a tremendous money making opportunity for yourself. And nothing can keep that business going better than a host of satisfied customers ready to spread the word about your quality services.

Gaining a foothold in the ever-expanding IT field can be daunting, but it can be done if you go about it the right way. One important factor is choosing the right areas to concentrate on. If you have the skills and knowledge to handle it, then opening a machine learning business may just be your best bet for guaranteed success.

CHAPTER 3: IMPACT OF MACHINE LEARNING TO THE PRODUCTIVITY

If there is one word that the enterprise wants to be associated with, it's "productive."

This is the metric that influences so many others by which business is measured -- success, efficiency, profit. And recently, artificial intelligence (AI) has been touted as a new way to increase productivity by replacing expensive workers with tireless machines. One recent example that has garnered media attention is the first demonstration of an autonomous big rig, the use of which could replace millions of truck drivers.

But AI has been getting a lot of undeserved limelight. Long before machines replace us, humans, they will be helping us to make smart decisions so we can become more productive -- autonomous machines be damned. This use of technology is called "intelligence augmentation, and because of its imminent and extensive impact, it deserves a closer look.

For many in the enterprise, artificial intelligence (AI) versus intelligence augmentation (IA) is a distinction without a difference. And certainly, that case can be made. In a Wall Street Journal op-ed, IBM president, chairman, and CEO Ginni Rometty points out that, whether you call them AI or IA, "these cognitive systems are neither autonomous nor sentient, but they form a new kind of intelligence that has nothing artificial about it. They augment our capacity to understand what is happening in the complex world around us."

This is true. But there is still a distinction to be made when it comes to maximizing productivity in the modern, data-diverse workplace. Applying either of these technologies to the wrong task will be counterproductive, however, advanced the application might be.

The "intelligence" provided by AI technology entails tapping into increasingly cheap computer processing power to evaluate alternate options more quickly than humans could. This is why AI-driven computers have been successful at playing chess, winning at Go, and even playing Jeopardy. Each of these tasks is characterized by the need to evaluate the best move from a finite set of options, however large that a number of options might be. Evaluating many options and learning from experience -- using a technology called machine learning -- is how artificial intelligence can pick the best outcome available.

But business decisions involve more than just evaluating many options. Business decisions involve ethics and intangibles, things that computers can't account for. That's where humans come in. And that is what is so compelling about IA. It enables humans to direct computers to evaluate options and then offer suggestions about what to do next. It is this type of cooperation between human and machine that will take humanity to the next level of productivity.

How does this work?

One practical example of exploiting machine intelligence to augment humans in an everyday business scenario is in collecting disparate information from a wide variety of apps, then employing intelligence augmentation technologies -- such as natural language processing and machine learning -- to automatically match related information. This could mean first collecting information from Salesforce, Dropbox, email, Office 365, Workday, and many other apps, then putting together related information in a puzzle-like fashion across all the apps so a human can see the information forest rather than getting lost in the data trees. This is an incredibly taxing cognitive process for humans, but a straightforward one for intelligent machines. With all the related information presented in a coherent context, the human can then make intelligent decisions about what to do next.

This doesn't mean that IA will supplant AI. Each use of intelligent technology has its place. Cases such as using chatbots to replace human operators will become more commonplace. Today, you can order food from Taco Bell via Slack or a pizza from Domino's using bots. These bots are handling the types of tasks that AI can manage more efficiently than a person because the context is defined and the degrees of decision-making it insufficient.

It's when the context becomes ambiguous, the decision criteria become fuzzy, and ethical considerations must be taken into consideration that AI falls short. It's here that intelligence augmentation can help people by coherently presenting information and options and letting the human take it from there. This is how machine intelligence will truly help organizations and individuals become more productive in the near- to mid-term, so this is where enterprises should be focused.

While artificial intelligence can improve efficiency by replacing humans for focused tasks, it is in the application of machine intelligence to augment human decision-making that the real increase in business productivity will occur. Understanding the roles machine learning can play is the key to maximizing both artificial and human intelligence in the enterprise.

By now, everyone and their grandparents are talking about machine learning and AI. Unfortunately, many people have been questioning whether all this effort is worth it, and some are worried about future job losses.

The hype and use a strategic goal, machine learning can offer real-world value. The increased ease, speed, and functionality it offers create avenues for use cases across the spectrum of industries that rely heavily on data.

For retail businesses, it provides an opportunity to improve and customize the customer experience. Let's take a look at five examples that are worth noting. Given that one of the world's most prolific scientific minds on AI just resigned from Baidu to focus on his next project that will "benefit the greater well," I felt this was timely.

Machine learning helping the disabled

Much like the closed captioning we've seen on TV, machine learning now makes it possible to identify specific elements from YouTube videos. New algorithms can visualize sound effects like applause, laughter, and music. This is a huge development for the versatility of the platform as it looks to become more accessible. Google's new video intelligence API made big news recently at Google Cloud Next, and it uses extremely high-tech models to identify specific elements in the video. This can include things as descriptive as a smile, water, or a species of animal. Machine learning makes these possible, and it opens the door for many new advances that will make online content more accessible for the disabled.

Student and startup employee Austin Lebetkin lives with autism spectrum disorder. He thinks that machine learning can open the door for the disabled to use and interact with digital content in many of the same ways that others do. Considering the amount of new content being developed that emphasizes audio-visual interactivity, this is a huge breakthrough for the disabled.

Suicide prevention

After some horrific events involving the live streaming of suicides, Facebook garnered a considerable amount of negative feedback. To combat the issue, the company decided to implement machine learning capabilities in the fight to prevent suicide. Machine learning will now "build predictive models to tailor interventions earlier." It's coming at the right time, considering there's been an increase in suicide rates over the past couple of years. With appropriate data mining, Facebook and others will be able to identify suicidal tendencies earlier and will be able to intervene more quickly.

Wearable medical devices

A company called Geneia is using machine learning to increase data efficiency and improve insights. By better-utilizing data, Geneia can improve medical status predictions at a much quicker rate. This means responses arrive earlier and contribute

To a higher quality of care. Clinical assessments and lab values used in the past are much less speedy and efficient. As a result of machine learning, there's a very real possibility that the sick or elderly can live more comfortably at home while reducing many of the risks associated with being away from medical facilities.

Student growth measures for success

Anyone who's studied in a public classroom knows that there are some different learning styles. Not everyone's brain functions the same, and everyone has different needs. Thanks to machine learning, meeting those needs is becoming much easier. Use of student-level projections allows for a standardized measure of success so that each student can learn and progress according to their characteristics. This creates a much higher chance for a student to respond positively and ultimately gives that student a better chance of learning.

Machine learning identifying skin cancer

Stanford researchers have been working very hard on this one. They've created a machine learning algorithm that uses a massive image database to make skin cancer diagnoses. Using the more recent developments combining deep learning with visual identification, the algorithm is aimed at replacing the initial observation step of skin cancer diagnosis. This will make the process easier and more efficient for both the patient and the doctor. Though the algorithm currently exists on a computer, there's a plan in place to expand to mobile very soon.

When you look at some of these cases, it's clear that there's a lot more at stake when we talk about the value of machine learning. Most of the buzzworthy tech news falls short of providing a sense of the huge potential at stake. Though current uses may seem simplistic, they are simply building blocks to begin using the technology in much more widespread, impactful ways. The companies mentioned here are finding new and creative ways to use machine learning, and it's these stories that deserve a much bigger place in the conversation surrounding AI.

CHAPTER 4: WAYS MACHINE LEARNING IS IMPROVING COMPANIES' WORK PROCESSES

Today's leading organizations are using machine learning-based tools to automate decision processes, and they're starting to experiment with more advanced uses of artificial intelligence (AI) for digital transformation. Corporate investment in artificial intelligence is predicted to triple in 2017, becoming a $100 billion market by 2025. Last year alone saw $5 billion in machine learning venture investment. In a recent survey, 30% of respondents predicted that AI would be the biggest disruptor to their industry in the next five years. This will no doubt have profound effects on the workplace.

Machine learning is enabling companies to expand their top-line growth and optimize processes while improving employee engagement and increasing customer satisfaction. Here are some concrete examples of how AI and machine learning are creating value in companies today:

Personalizing customer service

The potential to improve customer service while lowering costs makes this one of the most exciting areas of opportunity. By combining historical customer service data, natural language processing, and algorithms that continuously learn from interactions, customers can ask questions and get high-quality answers. In fact, 44% of U.S. consumers already prefer chatbots to humans for customer relations. Customer service representatives can step in to handle exceptions, with the algorithms looking over their shoulders to learn what to do next time around.

Improving customer loyalty and retention

Companies can mine customer actions, transactions, and social sentiment data to identify customers who are at high risk of leaving. Combined with profitability data, this allows organizations to optimize "next best action" strategies and personalize the end-to-end customer experience. For example, young adults coming off of their parents' mobile phone plans often move to other carriers. Telcos can use machine learning to anticipate this behavior and make customized offers, based on the individual's usage patterns before they defect to competitors.

Hiring the right people

Corporate job openings pull in about 250 résumés apiece, and over half of surveyed recruiters say shortlisting qualified candidates is the most difficult part of their job. Software quickly sifts through thousands of job applications and shortlists candidates who have the credentials that are most likely to achieve success at the company. Care must be taken not to reinforce any human biases implicit in prior hiring. But software can also combat human bias by automatically flagging biased language in job descriptions, detecting highly qualified candidates who might have been overlooked because they didn't fit traditional expectations.

Automating finance

AI can expedite "exception handling" in many financial processes. For example, when a payment is received without an order number, a person must sort out which order the payment corresponds to, and determine what to do with any excess or shortfall. By monitoring existing processes and learning to recognize different situations, AI significantly increases the number of invoices that can be matched automatically. This lets organizations reduce the amount of work outsourced to service centers and free up finance staff to focus on strategic tasks.

Measuring brand exposure. Automated programs can recognize products, people, logos, and more. For example, advanced image recognition can be used to track the position of brand logos that appear in video footage of a sporting event, such as a basketball game. Corporate sponsors get to see the return on investment of their sponsorship investment with detailed analyses, including the quantity, duration, and placement of corporate logos.

Detecting fraud. The typical organization loses 5% of revenues each year to fraud. By building models based on historical transactions, social network information, and other external sources of data, machine learning algorithms can use pattern recognition to spot anomalies, exceptions, and outliers. This helps detect and prevent fraudulent transactions in real time, even for previously unknown types of fraud. For example, banks can use historical transaction data to build algorithms that recognize the fraudulent behavior. They can also discover suspicious patterns of payments and transfers between networks of individuals with overlapping corporate connections. This type of "algorithmic security" applies to a wide range of situations, such as cyber security and tax evasion.

Predictive maintenance.

Machine learning makes it possible to detect anomalies in the temperature of a train axle that indicate that it will freeze up in the next few hours. Instead of hundreds of passengers being stranded in the

Countryside, waiting for an expensive repair, the train can be diverted to maintenance before it fails, and passengers transferred to a different train.

Smoother supply chains

Machine learning enables contextual analysis of logistics data to predict and mitigate supply chain risks. Algorithms can sift through public social data and news feeds in multiple languages to detect, for example, a fire in a remote factory that supplies vital ball bearings that are used in a car transmission.

Other areas where machine intelligence could soon be commonly used include:

Career planning

Recommendations could help employees choose career paths that lead to high performance, satisfaction, and retention. If a person with an engineering degree wishes to run the division someday, what additional education and work experience should they obtain, and in what order?

Drone- and satellite-based asset management

Drones equipped with cameras can perform regular external inspections of commercial structures, like bridges or airplanes, with the images automatically analyzed to detect any new cracks or changes to surfaces.

Retail shelf analysis

A sports drink company could use machine intelligence, coupled with machine vision, to see whether its in-store displays are at the promised location, the shelves are properly stocked with products, and the product labels are facing outward.

Machine learning enables a company to reimagine end-to-end business processes with digital intelligence. The potential is enormous. That's why software vendors are investing heavily in adding AI to their existing applications and in creating net new solutions.

But there are barriers to overcome. The most important are the availability of large quantities of high-quality data that can be used to train algorithms. In many organizations, the data isn't in one place or a useable format, or it contains biases that will lead to bad decisions. To prepare your enterprise for the future, the first step is to assess your existing information systems and data flows to distinguish the areas that are ready for automation from those where more investment is needed. Consider appointing a chief data officer to ensure that data is being properly managed as a corporate asset.

Prioritization

With so many opportunities, it can be hard to know where to start. To ease this burden, software providers are starting to offer predefined solutions enabled with state-of-the-art machine learning out of the box. Many organizations are also implementing AI centers of excellence to work closely with business departments. Wherever you start, it's important to link the projects to a long-term digital platform strategy to avoid having disconnected islands of innovation.

Cultural barriers

Many employees worry about the consequences of all of this technology on their roles. For most, it will be an opportunity to reduce tedious tasks and do more, but it's vital that employees have incentives to ensure the success of new machine learning initiatives. You'll also have to think carefully about customers. AI can augment the power to get insights from customer data -- perhaps beyond the point where customers are comfortable. Organizations must take privacy seriously, and relying on computers for important decisions requires careful governance. They should implement procedures to audit the real effects of any automated systems, and there should always be recourses and overrides as part of the processes. AI systems that use data about people should involve informed consent.

AI's continued rise is inevitable, and it's advancing into the workplace at a dizzying speed. The question now is not about whether managers should investigate adopting AI but about how fast they can do so. At the same time, organizations need to be thoughtful about how they apply AI to their organizations, with a full understanding of the advantages and disadvantages inherent in the technology.

Machine learning (ML) algorithms allow computers to define and apply rules which were not described explicitly by the developer.

There are quite a lot of articles devoted to machine learning algorithms. Here is an attempt to make a "helicopter view" description of how these algorithms are applied in different business areas. This list is not an exhaustive list of course.

The first point is that ML algorithms can assist people by helping them to find patterns or dependencies, which are not visible by a human.

Numeric forecasting seems to be the most well-known area here. For a long time computers were actively used for predicting the behavior of financial markets. Most models were developed before the 1980s, when financial markets got access to sufficient computational power. Later these technologies spread to other industries. Since computing power is cheap now, it can be used by even small companies for all kinds of forecasting, such as traffic (people, cars, and users), sales forecasting and more.

Anomaly detection algorithms help people scan lots of data and identify which cases should be checked as anomalies. In finance they can identify fraudulent transactions. In infrastructure monitoring they make it possible to identify problems before they affect business. It is used in manufacturing quality control.

The main idea here is that you should not describe each type of anomaly. You give a big list of different known cases (a learning set) to the system and system use it for anomaly identifying.

Object clustering algorithms allows to group big amount of data using wide range of meaningful criteria. A man can't operate efficiently with more than few hundreds of object with many parameters. Machine can do clustering more efficient, for example, for customers / leads qualification, product lists segmentation, customer support cases classification etc.

Recommendations / preferences / behavior prediction algorithms gives us opportunity to be more efficient interacting with customers or users by offering them exactly what they need, even if they have not thought about it before. Recommendation systems works really bad in most of services now, but this sector will be improved rapidly very soon.

The second point is that machine learning algorithms can replace people. System makes analysis of people's actions, build rules basing on this information (i.e. learn from people) and apply this rules acting instead of people.

First of all this is about all types of standard decisions making. There are a lot of activities which require for standard actions in standard situations. People make some "standard decisions" and escalate cases which are not standard. There are no reasons, why machines can't do that: documents processing, cold calls, and bookkeeping, first line customer support etc.

And again, the main feature here is that ML does not require for explicit rules definition. It "learns" from cases, which are already resolved by people during their work, and it makes the learning process cheaper. Such systems will save a lot of money for business owners, but many people will lose their job.

Another fruitful area is all kinds of data harvesting / web scraping. Google knows a lot. But when you need to get some aggregated structured information from the web, you still need to attract a human to do that (and there is a big chance that result will not be really good). Information aggregation, structuring and cross-validation, based on your preferences and requirements, will be automated thanks to ML. Qualitative analysis of information will still be made by people.

CHAPTER 5: Machine learning GROWTH AND TRENDS

Lots of market research reports say the global Machine Learning Chip Market is expected to attain a market size of $7.9 billion by 2022, growing at a CAGR of 9% during the forecast period. A major factor to the popularity of deep learning in the past is that we eventually reached a point whereby we experienced insightful real-world datasets and also abundant computational resources to precise coach huge, robust varieties on these types of datasets.

The needs of most recent programs, for instance, training as well as assumption for deep neural network varieties often requires exciting advancements in computer systems, at various degrees of the stack. Likewise, the design of fresh, strong hardware units is a superb encouragement and enabler for computing devices analysis. One particular primary factor approach to hasten machine learning examination is to have swift turnaround time on machine learning scientific tests.

The deep-learning software applications directing the current artificial intelligence revolution has largely run on relatively fundamental computer hardware. Some modern technology giants, for example, Google and Intel have centered a couple of their significant resources on putting together more specialty computer chips aimed at deep learning.

Deep learning's highly effective characteristics depend on algorithms called convolutional neural networks that are comprised of layers of nodes (also referred to as neurons). These kinds of neural networks could filter substantial amounts of info using their "deep" layers to emerge as more advantageous at, say, automatically determining unique human looks or comprehending various languages. These are the varieties of abilities that previously empower online services offered by major companies.

MACHINE-LEARNING is beginning to move up finance. A subset of artificial intelligence (AI) that excels at discovering formations together with helping to make estimations, it was previously the preserve of technology firms. The finance-related industry has jumped on the bandwagon.

Machine-learning is already much used for initiatives comparable to conformity, risk management, and fraudulent activity avoidance. Machine-learning is also good at automating financial decisions, whether assessing creditworthiness or eligibility for an insurance policy.

Machine-learning excels in spotting extraordinary variations of dealings, which might signify frauds. Businesses ranging from startups to behemoths offer these types of solutions.

While this is merely a short brief description, machine learning indicates you can make use of statistical models and probabilistic algorithms to answer questions consequently you can easily make educative decisions influenced by our data.

The fundamental assumption in Machine Learning is that analytical solutions can be built by studying past data models. Machine Learning supports that kind of data analysis that learns from previous data models, trends, patterns, and builds automated, algorithmic systems based on that study. This article takes a realistic look at where that data technology is headed into the future.

As Machine Learning relies solely on pre-built algorithms for making data-driven analysis and predictions, it claims to replace data analytics and prediction tasks carried out by humans. In Machine Learning, the algorithms have the capability to study and learn from past data, and then simulate the human decision-making process by using predictive analytics and decision trees.

The Two Drivers of Machine Learning Solutions: Raw Data and Data Models

On one side of Machine Learning are the raw data and on the other side the data models. Machine Learning enables data-driven decision systems to continuously learn from new data and adapt itself to deliver "reliable and repeatable" results. The newer technologies like Big Data and the Internet of Things have given a new leash to the traditional Machine Learning practices.

Some popular applications of Machine Learning are as follows:

Customer feedback for businesses on Twitter

Online recommenders in e-commerce sites such as Amazon or Netflix?

The self-driving Google Car

Fraud detection systems

Emerging Trends and Forecasts for Machine Learning

The variety of applications that Machine Learning supports includes search engines, image recognition, speech analysis, filtering tools, and robotics. The author of the article,

Where Machine Learning Is Headed, predicts that in the coming year, the global community will witness a tremendous growth of smart apps, digital assistants, and main-stream use of Artificial Intelligence. Machine Learning will proliferate the mobile market and enter the territories of drones and self-driving cars. Gartner's Ian Bertram predicts that more domain-specific and Machine Learning-enabled technologies will emerge this year. The democratization of AI/machine learning will continue, according to Mark Koh. The demand for making algorithms more easily available will push vendors to offer many new Machine Learning tools. Though such canned products will be available in the market, the skills required to fine tune existing algorithms, tweak the data, and develop an advanced model will remain in demand.

Gartner's Hype Cycle for Emerging Technologies

According to Gartner some new *"embryonic technologies"* will continue to increase regarding their market maturity:

People-Literate Technology or PLTs: They can hear a covert voice, or text messages into retainable intelligence will dominate personal communication and by 2020, about 40 percent people will use PLTs as the primary mode of technological interaction.

The Brain-Computer Interface: Claims to provide certain brain patterns to the computer for controlling a device or a program will also become popular.

Bioacoustics: These technologies are front-runners in the world of digital humanism that connects humans with digital businesses and workplaces. Apart from connected homes, smart robots, and self-driving cars, bioacoustics may also become important.

Some Important Observations about Machine Learning

The following observations on Machine Learning demonstrate many of its current uses and where various industry contributors believe it is going:

InfoWorld claims that though all Machine Learning technologies share the common goal of learning from past data to deliver improved results, the techniques to achieve that goal vary widely, from very simple techniques like linear or statistical regression to very complex ones like neural nets. Nowadays, the term "Machine Learning" is easily used as a marketing buzzword to differentiate competing products in the market.

According to Gartner's 2015 Hype Cycle Report of Emerging Technologies (also discussed above), Machine Learning only recently surfaced on Gartner's chart but has managed to surpass the expectations of its followers. In fact, Machine Learning has displaced and assumed the importance of Big Data. Big Data technologies have matured into mainstream business practices, and so no longer feature on the Hype Cycle.

Machine Learning is a new tool for better forecasting. In businesses, forecasting demand is increasingly becoming an insurmountable challenge, frequently leading to erroneous results and the trends in the demand data fluctuate so much, and the inherent causes behind those fluctuations are so complex that understanding demand variability is beyond the scope of most business leaders and managers. Moreover, manual factors intensify the human bias in demand planning activities. Now Machine Learning seems to offer a solution for demand forecasting. With the inherent capability to learn from current data, Machine Learning can help to overcome challenges facing businesses in their demand variations.

Wall Street is increasingly gearing up for newer technologies that will gradually control the fixed-income trading, block chains, and predictive analytics. McKinsey thinks that this trend will result in reduced manpower in the front and back offices. Global investment banks embracing automated trading will have a chance to increase their profits by at least 30 percent. A Wall Street insider feels the investment banking and trading businesses need more Data Scientists and Big Data Experts and fewer sales people and operators for continued success. This article also predicts that soon banks will embrace digital trading activities by partnering with tech startups.

In the recent Economic Forum at Davos, the data expert Andrew McAfee revealed that while the Industrial Revolution freed humans from manual labor, the Digital Revolution probably reduced the supremacy of the human brain. In Germany, an algorithm for reading street signs achieved a recognition rate of 99.4 percent, while that same rate for humans is only5 percent. According to Kaggle, the current Machine Learning algorithms are performing better than humans in domains, which were primarily dominated by humans. Google, Amazon, and Netflix are some of the large brands that are increasingly relying on Machine Learning rather than domain expertise to run their business operations.

CHAPTER6: How Machine Learning Keeps Retailers Ahead of Trends

As consumers increasingly reveal their shopping habits online, retailers can access social media, purchase history, consumer demand and market trends to understand their customers better, maximize spending and encourage repeat purchases. Retailers are considered early adopters of big data technology, integrating it into every imaginable business process to achieve a deeper understanding of consumers and associated buying trends.

To gain an in-depth understanding of the consumer, retailers need to access and analyze all available pertinent information. And while there's an unprecedented amount of data that retailers collect regarding consumer patterns, the ability to manage and my information from this data presents an overwhelming challenge.

Retailers are implementing technologies like Hadoop to build this big data solution, and quickly realizing that's only the start. They also need a solution that can make sense of the data in real time and provide insights that translate into tangible results, such as repeat purchasing.

Machine learning technology intelligently processes massive amounts of data and automates the analysis all the way through the supply chain to make this lofty goal possible.

In the hands of forward-thinking retailers, the possibilities for advanced machine learning are limitless, from sourcing, buying and supply chain all the way to marketing, merchandising and customer experience, retailers can make significant improvements by deploying a machine learning solution. Take the example of a company trying to predict what consumers will be buying next winter.

Machine learning algorithms can determine the availability of materials from outside vendors, incorporate predicted weather conditions that would affect transportation or create an increased need for outerwear, and recommend the quantity, price, shelf placement and marketing channel that would best reach the target consumer in a particular area. They can even incorporate volume-based or margin-based metrics to optimize sales based on individual store or corporate objectives.

You can hardly talk to a technology executive or developer today without talking about artificial intelligence, machine learning or bots.

While everyone agrees on the importance of machine learning to their company and industry, few companies have adequate expertise to do what they wanted the technology to do. Here are some insights into what we can expect in the coming years around ML and AI.

Every application is going to be an intelligent application

If your company isn't using machine learning to detect anomalies, recommend products or predict churn, you will start doing it soon. Because of the rapid generation of new data, availability of massive amounts of computing power and ease of use of new ML platforms.

Whether it is from large technology companies like Amazon, Google, and Microsoft or startups like Data), we expect to see more and more applications that generate real-time predictions and continuously get better over time. Of the 100 early-stage startups

Intelligent apps are built on innovations in micro-intelligence and middle-ware services.

Companies today fall into two categories (broadly): those that are building some form of ML/AI technology or those that are using ML/AI technologies in their applications and services. There is a tremendous amount of innovation happening in the building block services (aka, middle-ware services) that include both data preparation services and learning services or models-as-a-service providers.

With the advent of micro services and the ability to seamlessly interface with them through REST APIs, there is an increasing trend for the learning services and ML algorithms to be used and re-used — as opposed to having to be re-written from scratch over and over again.

For example, Algorithmic runs a marketplace for algorithms that any intelligent application can use as needed. Combining these algorithms and models with a specific slice of data (use-case specific within a particular vertical) is what we call micro-intelligence, which can be seamlessly incorporated into applications.

Trust and transparency are critical in a world of ML and AI

Several high-profile experiments with ML and AI came into the spotlight in the last year. Examples include Microsoft Tay, Google Deep Mind Alpha Go, Facebook M and the increasing number of Chabot of all kinds. The rise of natural user interfaces (voice, chat, and vision) provide very interesting options and opportunities for us as human beings to interact with virtual assistants (Apple Siri, Amazon Alexa, Microsoft Cortana and Viv).

There are also some more troubling examples of how we interact with artificial intelligence. For example, at the end of one online course at Georgia Tech, students were surprised to learn that one of the teaching assistants (named Jill Watson after the IBM Watson technology) with whom they were interacting throughout the semester was a Chabot and not a human being.

As much as this shows the power of technology and innovation, it also brings to mind many questions around the rules of engagement regarding trust and transparency in a world of bots, ML and AI.

A doctor or a patient will not be happy with a diagnosis that tells them they have a 75 percent likelihood of cancer, and they should use drug X to treat it. They need to understand which pieces of information came together to create that prediction or answer.

We believe that going forward we should have full transparency with regards to ML and think through the ethical implications of the technology advances that will be an integral part of our lives and our society moving forward.

There have been some conversations on whether we should be afraid of AI-based machines taking over the world. As much as advances in ML and AI are going to help with automation where it makes sense, it is also true that we will need to have human beings in the loop to create the right end-to-end customer experiences.

If your company isn't using machine learning to detect anomalies, recommend products or predict churn, you will start doing it soon.

At one point, Red fin experimented with sending ML-generated recommendations to its users. These machine-generated recommendations had a slightly higher engagement rate than users' search and alert filters. However, the real improvement came when Red fin asked its agents to review recommendations before they were sent out. After agents had reviewed the recommendations, Red fin was able to use the agents' modifications as additional training data, and the click-through rate on recommended houses rose significantly.

Splunk re-emphasized this point by describing how IT professionals play a key role in deploying and using Splunk to help them do their jobs better and more efficiently. Without these humans in the loop, customers won't get the most value out of Splunk.

Another company, Spare5, is a good example of how humans are sometimes required to train ML models by correcting and classifying the data going into the model. Another common adage in ML is garbage in, garbage out. The quality and integrity of data are critical to building high-quality models.

How can we control intelligent systems no one fully understands?

Machine learning is an integral part and critical ingredient in building intelligent applications, but the most important goals in building intelligent apps are to build applications or services that resonate with your customers, provide an easy way for your customer to use your service and continuously get better over time.

To use ML and AI effectively, you often need to have a large dataset. The advice from people who have done this successfully is to start with the application and experience that you want to deliver, and, in the process, think about how ML can enhance your application and what dataset you need to collect to build the best experience for your customers.

Machine Learning is a broader concept which includes classification of data, clusterization, supervised learning, unsupervised learning, building predictive modeling algorithms, etc. The application of Machine Learning is endless from self-driving cars, speech recognition to effective web search. Many compare Machine Learning to Statistics. While statistics focus on inference utilizing probabilistic models, Machine Learning is about predicting the outcome of the data provided.

One of the applications of Machine Learning in the RDMS world is to uncover the relationships among the tables. There are algorithms that you can use to uncover the relationships and gradually improve based on user's feedback. An important benefit of this is to bridge the lack of documentation for the databases. Once you've understood the data and the relationships, you can get started on data mining & conduct predictive analysis.

What is Predictive Analysis & why do you need it?

Predictive Analysis is the practice of extracting information from your existing data, determining patterns and then predicting the future outcomes or trends. Real-time and historical data is used for this purpose. It can enable firms to identify and respond to future opportunities better and quicker. It can identify the target customers, their behavior pattern, and time to communicate with them and thus the messaging to the prospective customers can be improved. Companies like Amazon and Netflix have used it brilliantly to create value for their customers and themselves. Predictive Analysis is, for example, useful for marketing and risk management.

Some common benefits/use cases of using Predictive Analysis are:

Incorporating sentiment in marketing analytics

Customer demand analysis and forecasting

Social analytics/sentiment (what is customer sentiment compared with competing products?)

Price optimization and analytics

Social network analysis (identifying the most influential product advocates)

Next best offer

Financial fraud detection

Machine learning has progressed dramatically over the past two decades, from laboratory curiosity to a practical technology in widespread Commercial use. Within artificial intelligence (AI), machine learning has emerged as the method of choice for developing practical software for

Computer vision, speech recognition, natural language processing, robot control, and other applications. Many developers of AI systems now recognize that, for many applications; it can be easier to train a system by showing it examples of desired input-output behavior than to program it manually by anticipating the desired Response for all possible inputs.

The effect of machine learning has also been felt broadly across computer science and across a range of industries concerned with data-intensive issues, such as consumer services, the diagnosis of faults in complex systems, and the control of logistic chains. There has been a similarly broad range of effects across empirical sciences, from biology to cosmology to social science, as machine-learning methods have been developed to analyze high throughput experimental data in novel ways

As a scientific endeavor, machine learning grew out of the quest for artificial intelligence. Already in the early days of AI as an academic discipline, some researchers were interested in having machines learn from data. They attempted to approach the problem with various symbolic methods, as well as what was then termed "neural networks"; these were mostly perceptions and other models that were later found to be reinventions of the generalized linear models of statistics. Probabilistic reasoning was also employed, especially in automated medical diagnosis.

However, an increasing emphasis on the logical, knowledge-based approach caused a rift between AI and machine learning. Probabilistic systems were plagued by theoretical and practical problems of data acquisition and representation. By 1980, expert systems had come to dominate AI, and statistics were out of favor. Work on symbolic/knowledge-based learning did continue within AI, leading to inductive logic programming, but the more statistical line of research was now outside the field of AI proper, in pattern recognition and information retrieval. Neural networks research had been abandoned by AI and computer science around the same time. This line, too, was continued outside the AI/CS field, as "connectionism," by researchers from other disciplines including

Hopfield, Rumelhart, and Hinton. Their main success came in the mid-1980s with the reinvention of back propagation.

Machine learning, reorganized as a separate field, started to flourish in the 1990s. The field changed its goal from achieving artificial intelligence to tackling solvable problems of a practical nature. It shifted focus away from the symbolic approaches it had inherited from AI, and toward methods and models borrowed from statistics and probability theory. It also benefited from the increasing availability of digitized information, and the possibility to distribute that via the Internet.

Machine learning and data mining often employ the same methods and overlap significantly, but while machine learning focuses on prediction, based on known properties learned from the training data, data mining focuses on the discovery of (previously) unknown properties in the data (this is the analysis step of Knowledge Discovery in Databases). Data mining uses many machine learning methods, but with different goals; on the other hand, machine learning also employs data mining methods as "unsupervised learning" or as a preprocessing step to improve learner accuracy. Much of the confusion between these two research communities (which do often have separate conferences and separate journals, ECML PKDD being a major exception) comes from the basic assumptions they work with: in machine learning, performance is usually evaluated with respect to the ability to reproduce known knowledge, while in Knowledge Discovery and Data Mining (KDD) the key task is the discovery of previously unknown knowledge. Evaluated on known knowledge, an uninformed (unsupervised) method will easily be outperformed by other supervised methods, while in a typical KDD task, supervised methods cannot be used due to the unavailability of training data.

Machine learning also has intimate ties to optimization: many learning problems are formulated as the minimization of some loss function on a training set of examples. Loss functions express the discrepancy between the predictions of the model being trained and the actual problem instances (for example, in classification, one wants to assign a label to instances, and models are trained to predict the pre-assigned labels of a set of examples correctly). The difference between the two fields arises from the goal of generalization: while optimization algorithms can minimize the loss of a training set, machine learning is concerned with minimizing the loss on unseen samples.

CHAPTER 7: PROS AND CONS OF MACHINE LEARNING

PROS

Feature learning

One of the interesting advantages of machine learning is that a system randomly initialized and trained on some datasets will eventually learn good feature representations for a given task. Classical approaches involved handcrafting features by an expert human. This took several years of painstakingly fine-tuning several parameters to get it right. Nowadays machine learning is used to discover relevant features in otherwise disordered datasets. Such features can be useful for things such as face detection, face recognition, speech recognition or image classification. Deep learning in particular aims to build higher-level abstract feature representation of data layer by layer. These features can be very powerful in speech and image recognition.

Parameter optimization

This is similar to feature learning as a group of tunable parameters can be visualized as a feature. Machine learning mostly employs a gradient based method of optimizing a large array of parameters. Again such parameters may be large in number, for example, a deep neural architecture can have billions of tunable parameters. These parameters when well set can result in a system working properly. It is not feasible for a human or humans to find such an optimal setting for a large number of parameters by hand. Thus large scale machine learning algorithms such as stochastic gradient descent are used to find an optimal setting.

It is used in the variety of applications such as banking and financial sector, healthcare, retail, publishing and social media, robot locomotion, game playing, etc.

It is used by Google and Facebook to push relevant advertisements based on users past search behavior.

It has capabilities to handle multi-dimensional and multi-variety data in dynamic or uncertain environments.

Due to machine learning, there are tools available to provide a continuous quality improvement in large and complex process environments.

Source programs such as Rapid miner helps in increased usability of algorithms for various applications.

Data Input from Unlimited Resources

Machine learning can easily consume unlimited amounts of data with timely analysis and assessment. This method helps review and adjusts your message based on recent customer interactions and behaviors. Once a model is forged from multiple data sources, it can pinpoint relevant variables. This prevents complicated integrations while focusing only on precise and concise data feeds. It allows time cycle reduction and efficient utilization of resources.

Fast Processing and Real-Time Predictions

Machine learning algorithms tend to operate at expedited levels. In fact, the speed at which machine learning consumes data allows it to tap into burgeoning trends and produce real-time data and predictions. For example, machine learning can optimize and create new offers for grocery and department store customers. This means that what customers might see at 1 p.m. may be different than what they see at 2 p.m.

In a nutshell, machine learning can identify, process and create data based on the following predictive analytics:

Customer leads conversion and revenue rates, buying and spending patterns.

Practical Scenarios

Meaningful impact

If you complete a successful machine learning project in the life sciences, you can change our understanding of the natural world. This can feel more meaningful than typical industrial applications of machine learning and can give you the motivation to follow through with the project.

Constant learning - You may have experience in either machine learning or life sciences, but it's unlikely that you have both. Doing an interdisciplinary project will force you to learn both topics.

Many Opportunities - After doing machine learning for computational biology, you can pivot to either computational biology or machine learning. When looking for a job in the industry, you will have experience for either computational biology jobs or machine learning jobs. You can explore both through an interdisciplinary project, and then decide which to focus on when applying to jobs.

New ideas - Applying machine learning methods to real-world data can open your eyes to the challenges of machine learning. Seeing the constraints and challenges of real-world data can inspire you to develop new, useful methods.

Applying machine learning to practical applications and scenarios is simply vital. While predictive analytics are instrumental in saving costs and building revenue - it is equally as important to understand their impacts on real-life situations pertaining to customer acquisitions or loss. No matter your business niche or market, the following tips will help you deal with these scenarios in a practical and engaging manner:

Churn analysis

it is imperative to detect which customers will soon abandon your brand or business. Not only should you know them in depth - but you must have the answers to questions like "Who are they? How do they behave? Why are They Leaving and What Can I do to keep them with us?". Churn analysis is what one uses to find which customers most probably will leave.

Customer leads and conversion

You must understand the potential loss or gain of any and all customers. In fact, redirect your priorities and distribute business efforts and resources to prevent losses and refortify gains. A great way to do this is by reiterating the value of customers in direct correspondence or via the web and mail-based campaigns. Customer defections to other brands - using recent data to identify your brand fallacies and product or service susceptibilities.

Customer defections - make sure to have personalized retention plans in place to reduce or avoid customer migration. This helps increase reaction times, along with anticipating any non-related defections or leaves. Machine Learning in the Medical Industry

Many hospitals use this data analysis technique to predict admissions rates. Physicians are also able to predict how long patients with fatal diseases can live. Similarly, medical systems are incorporating these technologies for cost-cutting measures, along with streamlining and centralizing expense reports and testing protocols. Experts even believe that radiologists will one day be replaced by computer algorithms that continuously churn and process data.

Machine Learning in the Insurance Industry

Insurance agencies across the world are also able to do the following:

- ✓ Predict the types of insurance and coverage plans new customers will purchase.
- ✓ Predict existing policy updates, coverage changes and the forms of insurance (such as health, life, property, flooding) that will most likely be dominant.
- ✓ Predict fraudulent insurance claim volumes while establishing new solutions based on actual and artificial intelligence. Sophisticated pattern recognition – Along with noting relationships, the Yottamine Predictive Platform can determine the type and quantify as well. This is not just happening with the key or even secondary

variables, but on every relationship that takes part in the pattern. This feature delineates irrelevant data as well, which provides the benefits of mitigating pre-processing requirements and accelerating processing. Since the solution has an ordering or ranking capability, the key variables self-identify as a part of the processing.

Intelligent decisions

Along with the capability to note irrelevant data, and rank the relative importance of variables, Yottamine will make decisions either aided by the user or not. This becomes apparent when modeling to predict a rare event. The solution can distinguish subclasses and make determinations on what data should be included and which shouldn't with very little instruction.

Self-modifying

Being able to tweak, add, or drop different aspects of an algorithm to better typify the data is a time saver. However, as this is also taking place to accommodate minor variables and sub-classes, so time demands are being held in check while the accuracy of the algorithm and its ability to predict are significantly improved.

Multiple iterations

As the model becomes more refined, YPP tests multiple iterations to produce a final version that delivers the highest level of accuracy while maintaining the best fit to the data.

Machine Learning Theory Analytics + Cloud

Yottamine is the first company to leverage the cloud as a source of high performance computing to drive advanced predictive analytics solutions. This enabled Yottamine to fully apply the most advanced thinking in Machine Learning Theory without compromise or cutting corners. The benefits of this approach make Yottamine the most intelligent choice for nearly all corporate Big Data needs.

Power

Having all the power you need, when you need it, means you have the power to drive the most intelligent predictive analytics solution available. Power also means running the volumes of data required for precise answers to your questions. No matter how you view Big Data, the power is there to extract the knowledge you need from your biggest and most challenging data.

Flexibility

Modeling and data mining projects come in all shapes and sizes, but typically, in setting up an in-house solution, cost considerations limit processing power to projects of average size. All of a sudden, planning isn't based on average and projects can become something far more than average.

Computing without Infrastructure

No Infrastructure limitations or a complicated distributed computing architecture to design, implement, and constantly monitor. Instead, have high-performance computing power available when you need it, for any number of projects necessary.

Cost Control

Meeting your BIG DATA requirements on a small data budget. Or let other business units manage their requirements on their small budget!

Kernel Based Learning and Support Vector Machines

Support Vector Machines (SVMs) represent the latest advancement in machine learning theory and deliver state of the art performance in numerous high value applications. Full scale SVMs have been difficult to put into production because such powerful procedures are resource intensive to compute.

The core of SVMs consists of a maximal margin hyperplane (also referred to as the decision boundary) and the use of a kernel function to transform the original data set into a high dimensional space (space for all possible combinations of predictive variables). The margin maximization principle has not only been proven mathematically to deliver robust and predictable performance on unseen data but also been shown to deliver state of the art performance on much real-world application. Massive data input from unlimited sources

Machine learning can consume virtually unlimited amounts of detailed data to constantly review and adjust your message based on very recent customer behaviors. Once a model is trained from a full set of data sources, it can identify the most relevant variables, limiting long and complicated integrations and allowing for focused data feeds.

Rapid processing, analysis, and predictions

The speed at which machine learning can consume data and identify relevant data makes the ability to act in real time a reality.

For example, machine learning can constantly optimize the next best offer for the customer, so what the customer might see at noon may be different than what that same customer sees at 1 PM.

Action systems

Those systems can act upon the outputs of machine learning and make the marketing message much more dynamic. For example, newly obtained information may suggest surfacing a retention offer to a specific customer. Or perhaps no offer at all if the behavior suggests the customer might not require one to create a conversion event.

Learning from past behaviors

A major advantage of machine learning is that models can learn from past predictions and outcomes, and continually improve their predictions based on new and different data. A simple example is whether the weather at a particular moment has a correlated effect on conversion behavior. Increases the Efficiency of Predictive Maintenance in the Manufacturing Industry

Manufacturing firms have corrective as well as preventive maintenance practices in place. However, these are often costly and inefficient. This is exactly where ML can be of great help. ML helps in the creation of highly efficient predictive maintenance plans. Following such predictive maintenance plans will minimize the chances of unexpected failures, thereby reducing unnecessary preventive maintenance activities.

Better Customer Segmentation and Accurate Lifetime Value Prediction

Customer segmentation and lifetime value prediction are the major challenges faced by marketers today. Sales and marketing units will have enormous amounts of relevant data sourced from various channels, such as lead data, website visitors and email campaigns. However, accurate predictions for incentives and individual marketing offers can be easily achieved with ML. Savvy marketers now use ML to eliminate guess work associated with data-driven marketing. For instance, using the data representing the behavioral pattern of a particular set of users during a trial period will help businesses in predicting the probability of conversion to paid version. Such a model triggers customer interventions to better engage the customers in the trial and also persuade customers to convert early.

Recommending the Right Product

Product recommendation is an important aspect of any sales and marketing strategy including upselling and cross-selling. ML models will analyze the purchase history of a customer and based on that they identify those products from your product inventory in which a customer is interested in. The algorithm will identify hidden patterns among the items and will then group similar products into clusters. This process is known as unsupervised learning, which is a specific type of ML algorithm. Such a model will enable businesses to make better product recommendations for their customers, thereby motivating product purchase. In this way, unsupervised learning helps in creating a superior Facilitates Accurate Medical Predictions and Diagnoses

In the healthcare industry, ML helps in easy identification of high-risk patients, make near perfect diagnoses, recommend best possible medicines, and predict readmissions. These are predominantly based on the available datasets of anonymous patient records as well as the symptoms exhibited by them. Near accurate diagnoses and better medicine recommendations will facilitate faster patient recovery without the need for extraneous medications. In this way, ML makes it possible to improve patient health at minimal costs in the medical sector.

Simplifies Time-Intensive Documentation in Data Entry

Data duplication and inaccuracy are the major issues confronted by organizations wanting to automate their data entry process. Well, this situation can be significantly improved by predictive modeling and machine learning algorithms. With this, machines can perform time-intensive data entry tasks, leaving your skilled resources free to focus on other value-adding duties.

Improves Precision of Financial Rules and Models

ML also has a significant impact on the finance sector. Some of the common machine learning benefits in Finance include portfolio management, algorithmic trading, loan underwriting and most importantly fraud detection. In addition, according to a report on 'The Future of Underwriting' published by Ernst and Young, ML facilitates continual data assessments for detecting and analyzing anomalies and nuances. This helps in improving the precision of financial models and rules.

Easy Spam Detection

Spam detection was one of the earliest problems solved by ML. A few years ago email providers made use of rule-based techniques to filter out spam. However, with the advent of ML, spam filters are making new rules using brain-like neural networks to eliminate spam mails. The neural networks recognize phishing messages and junk mail by evaluating the rules across a huge network of computers. Product-based Recommendation system.

CONS

As exciting as all these uses are, there are challenges with implementing machine learning in any organization. The first is simply understanding what kind of algorithm to use for the problem you need to solve. A clustering algorithm could be used to classify a restaurant customer as more likely to dine in than take out, but it can't be used to predict how raising menu prices would impact sales. Likewise, a regression algorithm would be able to address the effect of price changes on sales, but can't predict one of a closed set of outcomes.

There's also a risk of "over fitting" the data, which is simply training the system to understand a set of data so well that it loses the ability to generalize, learn, and make predictions based on new data. In this case, the model tends to make inconsistent predictions and becomes worthless.

Also, some problems may not be solvable with machine learning. Unfortunately, you can't always predict which can be solved, so the process of applying machine learning to the data never ends, leading an organization to chase the problem but never develop a functional model. In this case, the solution is knowing when to quit trying.

Acquisition of relevant data is the major challenge. Based on different algorithms data need to be processed before providing as input to respective algorithms. This has the significant impact on results to be achieved or obtained.

Interpretation of results is also a major challenge to determine the effectiveness of machine learning algorithms.

Based on which action to be taken and when to be taken, various machine learning techniques are needed to be tried.

Next level to machine learning technology is being researched.

Works with continuous loss functions

Non-differentiable discontinuous loss functions are hard to optimize using machine learning techniques. There are several reasons why discontinuous loss functions are important. In cases such as sparse representations, discontinuous loss functions can help to find such sparse representations. In many cases, such non-differentiable loss functions are approximated by smooth loss functions without much loss in sparsity.

Limited

It is not a guarantee that machine learning algorithms will always work in every case imaginable. Sometimes or most of the times machine learning will fail, thus it requires some understanding of the problem at hand in order to apply the right machine learning algorithm.

Large data requirements

Some machine learning algorithms need a lot of training data such as deep learning algorithms. It might be cumbersome to work with or collect such large amounts of data. Fortunately, there are a lot of

PETER van DIJCK

training data for image recognition purposes. Noisy Datasets - Many life science datasets rely on inaccurate experimental techniques to gather data. While most machine learning methods can overcome noisy unbiased sampling, the experimental methods in the life sciences can be biased, introducing a challenge for machine learning methods. Furthermore, the bias of the measurements is unknown and thus cannot be easily corrected. In practice, this lowers the accuracy of most machine learning methods when applied to datasets from the life sciences.

Small sample sizes

While computational biology is transitioning to the paradigms of big data, current datasets are often larger in some features than the number of samples. This limits the types of machine learning approaches that can be used.

Difficulty evaluating accuracy

Because the truth is unknown (biology is an unsolved problem), it can be difficult to evaluate how good a machine learning method is. For example, imagine you write a machine learning approach to predict which genes are important in cancer. Because we do not know the answer, it is difficult to evaluate how well your machine learning method works.